BEGINNER'S GUIDE TO RUNNING

The Definitive Guide On How To Start Running & Discover The Runner In You

By Kanisk Nayan

Kanisk Nayan

Table of Contents

BEGINNER'S GUIDE TO RUNNING	1
The Definitive Guide On How To Start Running & Discover The Runner In You	1
DISCLAIMER	4
ABOUT THE AUTHOR	6
PREFACE	7
INTRODUCTION	10
My story	10
It's All About 'Why'	14
The First Step	16
The History of Marathon	17
Types of marathon	18
We are born runners!!!	20
Evolution	20
Realistic expectations from running	21
RUNNING AS A LIFESTYLE	25
"Fitness is not a goal, it is a lifestyle."	25
Why I support running as a lifestyle	25
HOW TO ENJOY YOUR RUNS	28
BEST TIME TO RUN	32
Importance of no schedule	32
Importance of schedule	34
USEFUL TOOLS	35

BEGINNER'S GUIDE TO RUNNING

Shoes	35
Mobile Apps	36
Gears	38
CORRECT RUNNING POSTURE	**43**
Importance of breathing properly	43
Posture	44
Before a run:	45
During a run:	46
After a run:	47
MOTIVATION	**48**
How much do you need?	48
DIET	**51**
What to eat and what not to eat?	51
What to eat after a run?	54
Hydration	56
CROSS-TRAINING	**59**
INJURIES	**61**
No pain no gain	63
REGISTERING FOR HALF-MARATHON	**64**
Declaration to the world	64
Take help from support groups	64
Training for half-marathon	65
Taking the first step (schedule)	66
FINAL WORDS FROM THE AUTHOR	**69**
Realistic expectations from running:	69
THANK YOU	**71**

DISCLAIMER

The guidance contained in this book is for informational purposes only. I am neither a medical practitioner nor a professional trainer. Any health advice that I provide is my opinion, based on my own experience and research.

You are advised to seek the advice of a professional doctor or a trainer before acting on something that I have published or recommended. Please understand that there are some affiliate links contained in this guide that I may financially benefit from. The material in this guide may include information, products or services by third parties. Third Party Materials comprise of the products and opinions expressed by their owners. As such, I do not assume responsibility or liability for Third Party materials or opinions. The publication of such Third Party Materials does not constitute my guarantee of any information, instruction, opinion, products or services contained within the Third Party Material. The use of recommended Third Party Material does not guarantee any success related to your fitness or health benefits. Publication of such Third Party Material is simply a recommendation and an expression of my own opinion of that product/material.

No part of this publication shall be reproduced, transmitted, or sold in whole or in part in any form, without the prior written consent of the author. All trademarks and registered trademarks appearing in this guide are the property of their respective owners. Users of this guide are advised to do their own due diligence when it comes to making fitness decisions and all information, products, services that have been provided should be independently verified by yourself or your own qualified fitness professionals. By reading this guide, you agree that I am not responsible for the success or failure of your fitness decisions relating to any information presented in this guide.

ABOUT THE AUTHOR

"A writer only begins a book. A reader finishes it."
- Samuel Johnson (English writer)

Brought up in Bokaro (India), Kanisk Nayan is a fitness enthusiast. He has a passion for inspiring people to lead a healthy lifestyle and achieve their fitness goals. Kanisk ran his first official half-marathon in 2015 and has never given up on running ever since. He is a banker by the day and founder of the popular running website, https://www.madoverrunning.com/.

In his spare time, he likes to watch superhero movies and traveling across the globe. Follow Kanisk Nayan on Twitter (@kanisknayan).

PREFACE

"A journey of a thousand miles begins with a single step"
- Lao-Tzu (ancient Chinese philosopher and writer)

In the year 1966, a book named 'Jogging' was published in America which was co-authored by the co-founder of Nike, Bill Bowerman and it introduced to the world a new hobby, recreational running. Approximately 25 million people had taken up jogging in the 1970s. It was an instant craze and many celebrities were part of this. I invite you to be part of this worldwide craze. The origin of running dates back to thousands of years, details of which I will cover in a later chapter.

So, what is running? Running can be defined as a movement in which the speed is more than walking and in doing so one or both the feet are off the ground. If imagined, you will start sensing an adrenaline rush. Not feeling it yet? You will feel it soon.

If you are not a runner and aim to run a half marathon (or any other distance) in distant future, then I would congratulate you for being courageous enough to even think about it. This is a bold thought and you should be proud of yourself. Having said that, I strongly believe that before anyone starts their training for half-marathon (or any other distance); some prior experience of running is required. Your body has to be physically ready to start the training. Say, for example, you wish to start with the half-marathon training. For a beginner, half-marathon training may seem challenging. You have to run long distances frequently and be regular every week. It may appear to be a humongous task for a first-time runner based on the mere fact that it is your first time. Good news is that it would only be a matter of time before you get used to such distances. To help you on this journey, I have covered as many relevant topics that will prepare you both physically and mentally before starting any sort of distance training.

Before picking up this book, you may have an idea of what you wish to achieve by running. It could be as ambitious as competing in your first half-marathon or could simply be an idea of developing a new hobby. Throughout this book, I have included tools and tips which will help you kick-start your running journey to achieve your aim. Through this book, I intend to provide you with the proper education so that you make the least number of mistakes. In 2015, I spent hours in front of my laptop trying to learn as much as possible about running and specifically half-marathon, from history to proper running posture to a proper diet. I have poured all my knowledge about running in this book. You will get to know things which I did right and hopefully, learn from my mistakes which I recommend you to avoid.

Running a half-marathon is as crazy as it sounds. 13.1 miles (21.04 km!), is quite a distance, to be honest. It takes focused training and discipline. It's important for you to understand that it is more of a mental sport than it is a physical sport. With the right frame of mind, getting physically ready is not a mammoth task.

While writing this book, I have assumed that you have no prior running experience (or not much). I have designed this book to help you reach a level where you can start the training for half-marathon. For your reference, I have provided few resources as well in the book which can guide you on how to train for half-marathon.

Consider this book as a <u>logical first step</u> before starting your half-marathon (or 5K/10K) training. By the time you have read it all, you can boast of a knowledge which only experienced runners have.

No matter how you discovered this book, I am glad that you have found it. I have written this book with only one intention in mind – **to help you start your running journey in the least troublesome way**. Please remember that you are not reading a formula but a guide. The purpose of any guide is to help you reach a particular goal. The most important thing to remember is that a guide succeeds only when the reader makes the most out of it. In this story, the lead character is played by you.

My only wish is that this guide helps you begin the running journey you have always dreamt of. I salute your willingness to bring a positive change in your life.

If at any point you have any questions while reading this book, please reach out to me on Twitter (@kanisknayan). Even if you don't have any questions, just visit my twitter handle to say hello! If you want to reach out to me personally you can send a private message on Twitter.

INTRODUCTION

"The secret of getting ahead is getting started."
- Mark Twain (American writer)

My story

Well, before I plunge into the details of how to train and prepare yourself before half-marathon training, I would take this opportunity to introduce myself and help you understand why I feel I am qualified enough to teach you something about long-distance running.

I am a regular Indian guy and as of today (September 2016), I am only a few months away from turning 30. I work for a highly reputed multinational bank and have been in the industry for quite some time now. In April 2013, I moved to New Delhi (India's capital). New Delhi is a fast-paced metro city with individuals from all corners of the world.

Someday in the month of June 2013, I saw an advertisement of Delhi Half-marathon in the daily newspaper. It was scheduled for the month of November that year.

I had a small desire to run but I had my own mental blocks. Let me be honest with you - I had never been a runner in my life, never ever! As a teenager, I sucked at long distance races, especially mini-marathons. A long time ago, when I was in high school, every winter all the grades had to run mini-marathons, named the 'Cross-Country'. Distances used to be in the range of 3 to 5 km. In one of those years, I was the last person to cross the finish line. I remember all my friends cheering me up and pushing me to run faster. It was certainly an embarrassing moment for me. Next year, I was determined that no matter what I would not be the last person to cross the finish line. I trained for a week and that year and on the race day, I was second to last to cross the finish line. Damn! I thought maybe I was not a runner at all and it would never ever be my cup of tea. I had given up on running forever. Even in college, when I used to play football, I hated running. You can very well conclude that running was not my forte.

In 2013, when I saw the half-marathon advertisement, I got excited. Maybe, this was my chance to prove that I could be a runner as well. I kept thinking about it for next few days. I just couldn't think of anything else. Even after so much of overthinking, I didn't register that year. Mere thinking is not sufficient, execution is more important. Hundreds of people spend endless hours thinking and planning for the goals they want to achieve. Only the doers get the chance to share their success stories.

Next year, in 2014, I saw the advertisement again. I researched a bit about proper training and came to the conclusion that I didn't have sufficient time left for training. Therefore, very conveniently, I skipped it again that year.

The summer of 2015 was different. An Indian supermodel, [Milind Soman](#) completed Ironman Challenge in Switzerland. It was all over the social media and TV news channels. For your information, the 'Ironman Challenge' is one of the toughest triathlon challenges in the world. It comprises of 3.8 km of swimming, 42.2 km of running and 180.2 km of cycling. All of these tasks are required by the participants to be completed within a timeframe of 16 hours. Milind Soman completed this challenge in 15 hours and 19 minutes. Now, here is the interesting part - He was 50 years old at that point of time. When I read about it, I put down the newspaper in awe and told myself, "Come on Kanisk! If Milind at the age of 50 years can successfully complete Ironman Challenge, why can't you run a simple half-marathon?"

(Quick update - In February 2017 he achieved another feat as he completed Florida's Ultraman challenge, just double the distances mentioned in Ironman Challenge.)

Out of excitement, I researched online all I could about running a half-marathon. In an ocean of information available online, it is easy to get lost. One day, I simply decided it was about time to kick off my first ever half-marathon training. The day registrations got opened for the Delhi half-marathon, I enrolled myself. I was more than ready this time.

Once I started training, I faced both physical and mental challenges. I had to educate myself regularly on various aspects of distance running. Trust me, I doubted myself every alternate day and wanted to quit hundreds of times. After a few months of not so perfect physical and mental training, the day of half-marathon was near. A night before the race day, I was both excited and nervous and therefore couldn't sleep properly.

It was a mild cold November morning. Thousands of participants had turned up. Few celebrities also graced the occasion and were motivating runners at the start line. A few hours later, that Sunday morning, before most of my friends and family members woke up; I had successfully run my first official half-marathon. I took 2 hours and 48 minutes to complete it. Not an ideal timing but I am still glad I did it.

Check this [link](https://www.madoverrunning.com/about) (or visit https://www.madoverrunning.com/about if you are reading a paperback) and you will see the smile on my face after receiving the medal. Trust me I couldn't have given a better smile. I can't exactly define the feeling but I had never been so proud of myself. It was a wonderful experience and I still beam with a smile when I think of crossing the finishing line.

I was on cloud nine and was feeling on top of the world. To celebrate it, I headed to a nearby bar with a friend and had my favourite beer. Later that night, I read that post-marathon, alcohol intake should be avoided as the body is already dehydrated and alcohol doesn't help in recovering! *facepalm*

I had committed many mistakes both during half-marathon training and post-race and yet I am proud that I did it. If you are wondering, how I did it in my first attempt then the answer is simple - I trained well (maybe not so perfect).

I will teach you everything you should know before starting your half-marathon training. At the end of the book, I have included a simple training plan which you can start using straight away. I would advise you to start with this training plan at least 1-2 months prior to starting half-marathon training. The training plan provided at the end is designed for fairly new runners or someone who has no experience of running. <u>Getting used to running is the critical first step</u>. Training for a half-marathon is the next logical step. This book is about mastering the first step. By the end of this book, you will be fully equipped and ready to start your running journey.

It's All About 'Why'

Let me start with a very powerful word - WHY!

I am sure you must have heard numerous times in your life the importance of 'why' before figuring out 'what, how and where'. The word 'Why' has the power to fuel 'what, how and where'. Knowing your 'why' will bring you out of the self-doubting moments and also the times when you would want to quit running. I can assure you from my experience that there will many such moments.

Now is the time to do some self-talk and ask yourself the most important question of all – *"Why do you want to run?"*

Is it to lose weight?

Is it to increase stamina?

Do you have the desire to run a half-marathon?

Or is it simply to get fit?

No matter what the answer is, trust me, you can achieve it.

Remember this book is about you and how 'you' can become a better runner. So, let's take a moment and think about your 'why'.

What is the first 'why' that comes to your mind? My advice is not to proceed further without thinking about your 'why'.

Assuming you have thought of a reason, let us find the core reason, to make your 'why' even stronger. We will use a technique which has been successfully used by thousands of people to find the reason which is fiery hot.

The 5 Whys: Designed by Sakichi Toyoda, the founder of Toyoda Industries Corporation, the primary it was developed was to find the underlying reason of any problem in Toyota factories. The answer to each question leads to the next why. The answer to the previous why is the question for the next why. Confused? Let me show you an example.

E.g. Let us assume that we have an imaginary friend - Tom. He wants to run. Let us try to find the underlying reason.

Question 1: Hey Tom, why do you want to run?

Answer 1: I want to lose weight.

Question 2: Why do you want to lose weight?

Answer 2: I want to look good.

Question 3: Why do you want to look good?

Answer 3: A few years ago, I gained 30 kgs. My confidence is on a decline ever since. I have lost all of my self-confidence.

In the above case, it's pretty evident, that for Tom, the underlying reason for losing weight is to feel confident again. By running regularly, this is what he hopes to achieve.

I stopped at 3rd why. Often times, you will find that the critical why will be answered in 3rd or 4th why. 5th level depth is not required in most of the cases. You are the best judge. Stop whenever you feel the reason is compelling enough for you. I request you not to go nuts about it and go on to 20th why.

Well, go ahead and find your why. My why was simple - to 'bring out the runner in me.' Yes, with time, reasons can change. It's different and deeper now.

Have you found your underlying why yet?

The First Step

If you are not a regular runner, then, in that case, let's take a moment and decide the date when you are going to start running regularly.

Don't confuse it with the start date of your half-marathon training. I am simply asking you to decide the date when you will start running regularly. Choose the date as per your convenience. Think well. If required, go through your schedule and then decide. For the sake of momentum, don't choose a date one year from now.

Just in case you are already running regularly, I would like to congratulate you and I'm confident this book will help you with many new useful information in order to become a better runner and enjoy it even more.

Coming back to first time runners; now that you have thought of a date, write it down somewhere or mark it in your phone's calendar. Alternatively, you can write it in the space provided below.

This section is advisable for first-time runners. As mentioned earlier, I believe that before starting with half-marathon training, it's important to get used to running and let your body adjust to this new form of exercise. Please refer to the training plan that you have provided at the end of the book. Let us assume that you are going to follow the training plan for approximately 2 months. Once you have followed the schedule for 2 months, you will have graduated to a new physical and mental state and would be ready to start with half-marathon training. In general, half-marathon training lasts approximately 3 months. So, in total, we are looking at almost 5 months of the training plan. You can always customize (add or subtract) the number of days from the training plan in this book as per your current fitness level. To help you plan, answer the below questions and you will have a rough schedule for you to follow.

Question 1: On which date are you are going to start running? (not half-marathon training)

Answer 1: DD/MM/YYYY (e.g. 1/1/2017)

Question 2: What date are you going to start half-marathon training?

Answer 2: Answer 1 + 2 months (e.g. 1/1/2017 + 2 months = 1/3/2017)

For even better understanding, in the above example say you have decided to start running regularly from 1/1/2017. Add two months to it and you have the start date of your half-marathon training, i.e. 1/3/2017.

The above-mentioned dates are examples only and actual dates will vary.

The History of Marathon

How about a bit of a history class?

The story of the origination of marathon is very old. It is said that in 490 BC, the Greeks had a victory over the Persians. A soldier named Pheidippides ran all the way from the battlefield near a town in Greece named Marathon, to Athens, the capital of Greece.

He ran close to 25 miles (approximately 40 km) to announce the victory. Unfortunately, soon after announcing the news, the exhausted messenger died.

The world started following 25 miles distance in the memory of this event for all marathons. The distance was then changed to 26.2 miles and is currently the official distance for a full marathon. The distance was extended by 1.2 miles in 1908 games in London so that the race could start from the lawns of Windsor Castle. This was done so that the royal kids could watch the start from their windows. Talk about the perks of being a royal kid!

Hence, the distance for a full marathon is 26.2 miles and that for a half-marathon is 13.1 miles.

Today, thousands of people run both forms of marathon every year. Of the two, half-marathon is more popular.

Types of marathon

In general, there are 3 popular types of long distance runs (In descending order of distance):

1. Ultramarathon - More than 50 miles or 80 km
   It would be not wrong to say that any running distance higher than the traditional marathon distance can be termed as an ultramarathon.

2. Full marathon - 26.2 miles or 42.17 km
   This form of the marathon has been accomplished by thousands of people till date. There are many aspects to

focus on when training for full-marathon - diet, following a proper training plan and rest.

3. <u>Half marathon</u> - 13.1 miles or 21.08 km:
Half-marathon has emerged as a more popular running format as compared to others. You have to run a substantial yet not so challenging distance. Half the distance yet double the fun. It is not a humongous task to finish half-marathon within 3 hours. As a beginner, you can comfortably aim to complete a half-marathon run. I have done it in my first year. For a newbie runner, it is surely a challenge but if you plan and train properly, then, it can be accomplished. I will share few training resources in the coming sections.

4. <u>Other formats</u> - 10km run, 5km run, and the likes. As a novice runner, you can first attempt few 5k/10k run and then gradually go on to run your first half-marathon.

I started my running journey with a half-marathon and I am happy about the decision. Even though I was never a runner, my involvement in sports, like football, lawn tennis or cycling had definitely helped. I decided to jump straight into half-marathon training. Honestly, it wasn't the brightest idea and I guess it would have been better if I had gotten my body used to running before starting the training. I had to face a fair number of physical and mental challenges. Please don't feel discouraged by my words; all I want you to do is decide for yourself based on your current fitness level.

We are born runners!!!

Yes, that is true. Don't compare yourself with other mammals like horses or dogs. We are unique in our own way. Just remember a simple statement - *We are born runners!*

Of all the tips and tools that I will be sharing with you, this is the most critical one. The tip is to be mentally prepared. In the next few paragraphs, I will try to convince you that we are meant to be runners and will back it up with scientific or logical reasoning.

Human beings are born to run. Our bodies, over a long period of time, have evolved so that we can run well.

Evolution

1. We have a straight spine. We don't slouch while walking or running. If we were meant to run fast, then the design would support aerodynamics, as seen in a horse or a dog. We are built to run slow long distances.

2. Let's look at the structure of our feet. We are always well-balanced on our feet. While running, our bodies can carry forward 50% of the energy from the last stride. Isn't that an efficient way to run?

3. We sweat through our skin which controls the body temperature. We don't pant to control the temperature through saliva which is common in most of the mammals. This design is helpful because our windpipe is free for inhaling oxygen-rich air.

So, we have a straight spine, a well-balanced body structure and a temperature control system in place - perfect ingredient for long distance runs. That's evolution for you! All we need to do is to tap the full potential of our body.

A long time ago, when we used to kill animals in forests for food, as human beings, we had many technical disadvantages like weaker claws, blunt teeth, and so on and so forth. Therefore, we simply chased our prey till the point they got tired. Then, we used to hit tired animals with rocks and killed them. The exhausted animals had no energy to fight back. We killed by running!

Hope you are a bit convinced by now. After reading and knowing all of these facts/logics, I could feel a different sense of satisfaction while running. At the back of my mind, I used to tell myself that running is a normal activity. I am doing what is expected out of me. With time all pain will be gone and running would become a natural way of commuting. Let me know if you can sense something similar while running as well.

Realistic expectations from running

As part of half-marathon training, I had to run quite a lot. In the last 3-4 weeks, I was running an average of 30-35 miles per week. Below I have shared my observations after few days/weeks of running. Hope this will help you set realistic expectations for running and in doing so any or all possible future disappointments will be avoided.

Am I being overprotective? Probably yes, but at the same time, I want you to enjoy running along with its entire process and be mindful of what is in store for you.

What will running do?

1. Running will increase your stamina multiple times - As we start running regularly, our body adjusts to the new regime. Stamina is the ability to continue with an activity for an extended period of time. With time, your running stamina increases and you are able to run further, week after week. The difference can also be felt in the daily activities. Few weeks down the training plan, I could walk more, climb more stairs, dance more, work more and certainly, run more. The confidence which you develop from increased stamina is priceless. You are always full of energy.

2. You will lose extra body fat - As expected, you will start losing any extra flab, your body will start looking leaner and your legs will look toned. Body fat is the energy not consumed by us and therefore it is stored as a reserve. Only after 20 minutes into any workout, your body starts burning any stored fat.

3. Increase in cardiovascular stamina - Cardiovascular stamina is the ability of heart, lungs and blood cells to provide oxygen to various body parts. An optimal supply of oxygen means better productivity. Running regularly definitely helps in achieving this.

4. Increase in metabolism - Metabolism refers to the various chemical processes performed by our body to maintain the living condition of cells and the organisms. While running, your body's metabolism increases to provide sustained energy. Our body needs calories at the time of running. A very good source of instant energy is the stored fat in our bodies.

5. You will be able to walk endlessly and climb stairs effortlessly - I went for a vacation to Malaysia in 2016 and had to walk close to 15-20 km every day. This included numerous flights of stairs as well. It was my observation, unlike my co-travelers, I never got

tired. Be it morning, noon, evening or late night, I was always on fire. Always ready to move around. All of the credit goes to running regularly.

6. You subconsciously start eating healthy food - Once you start working out regularly, irrespective of the type of exercise, it's normal for anyone to keep a check on their eating disorders. The interesting part is that you don't have to put a lot of effort into it as well. I have seen multiple times, that as soon as I get serious about working out, I automatically also get serious about eating right. In my head, I am always talking to myself and telling myself that it's a bad idea to ruin my running efforts by eating unhealthy food. It's simple math, energy used should be equivalent to the energy consumed in the form of food. Imagine two scenarios. First, you are eating a lot of junk food daily and not working out. That is a sure shot way to gain weight. In the second scenario following the same diet but accompanying it with regular workouts. You will still not be very healthy as your diet mostly includes junk but at the same time, you won't become as fat as in the first case. Eat healthy, workout regularly, rest well, and repeat. I will share details on good eating habits in a later section.

7. There will be a glow on your face - During a run, as you sweat; all the dirt and oil on the face are washed away. It acts like a mini facial. Your face automatically glows, just another perk of running.

8. New confidence - Running regularly comes with many benefits. A new sense of confidence is one of those. At an age when physical activities are on a decline, competing for and completing a half-marathon (even 5k run) is an accomplishment in itself. The time and energy dedicated to training bring a new purpose in life. Once you complete any form of run, be it 5k, 10k or a half-marathon, you will start feeling more confident about yourself.

Physical achievements are mental achievements as well. Think about it - You conquered your fears and pain, challenged yourself on regular basis and met your end goal. Isn't that powerful. For at least few months, everyone around you (including yourself) will refer to your running achievement and keep you motivated. Don't be surprised if people look up to you for some inspiration as well. You feel humbled by such recognition.

RUNNING AS A LIFESTYLE

"Fitness is not a goal, it is a lifestyle."

I am sure you must have heard or read the above statement sometime in your life. It is absolutely true. Staying fit should not be the end goal, but the way of your life. It is absolutely alright if you want to choose cycling or swimming or want to hit the gym over running. Your goal should not just be to get fit but also maintain it. Include any sort of workout as part of your daily lifestyle. That is a worthy goal. Don't be obsessed about it but at the same time, it should be your top 2-3 priority in life. Exercise regularly, eat healthy food, take proper rest and have fun in life.

I am in love with running. I can't imagine going back to a stage when I used to dread it. I have crossed that stage and want to be in this physical and mental state as long as I can. I have tried many other sports and workouts but running brings a different sense of satisfaction. Let me share my reasons.

Why I support running as a lifestyle

1. Free! Free! Free! - Who doesn't like free stuff? The day you want to start running you can start with it. No questions asked. Just go out and start running. Even if you don't have a good pair of running shoes, you can simply go out and run barefoot on grass. It is that simple.

2. Easy to start (downside: easy to quit as well) - It is like starting a blog of your own, easy to start, easy to quit. Discipline plays an

important role. If you are ready to invest time and energy into it, over a period of time you will see positive results.

3. No location constraint - You can go out for a run <u>anywhere</u> in the world. All you need is a desire to run. I have run on vacations and on business trips. Now I always keep a section in my travel bag dedicated to running shoe and sportswear so that I can continue with my daily runs wherever I go. It is fun to explore a new city on foot. It is difficult to carry your cycle everywhere; you can't be sure if your hotel has a swimming pool and you can't definitely carry your gym equipment.

4. No time constraint - Think about it. You can go out to run anytime you want. If you have a safe locality, you can go out to run even at night. I have run at 5 o'clock in the morning and as late as 11 o'clock at night.

5. Low/No equipment required - Apart from comfortable sportswear and a good pair of shoes, no other equipment is needed. Running is one of the simplest exercises you can ever do.

A piece of advice: Staying fit brings many positive changes in your life. Right from the way you think about the way you do things in normal life. The confidence which you build over a period of time because of staying fit is reflected in all other aspects of life. On the other hand, at times of physical/mental stress, just to know that at least your body will support you gives a feeling of satisfaction. Your body is the only place your soul stays, so, please take care of it. Remember the age-old saying, healthy, wealthy and wise? You will always be proud to lead a healthy lifestyle. In a later chapter, I will share tips on how to make running a part of your normal life. It's going to be fun :)

Now that you have understood the basics of mental preparation required for running, let's start looking at other aspects as well. I have been running regularly for a few years now and over a period of time, I have learned many great things about running. Experience teaches you a lot of things. The best part about reading a book or listening to an experienced runner is that in a very short span of time you can learn various things without spending the same time yourself. Read the next few sections carefully so that you can gain as much knowledge as possible. In case of any queries, you can always reach out to me.

HOW TO ENJOY YOUR RUNS

"From enjoyment comes the will to win."
- Arthur Lydiard (former New Zealand runner and coach)

When you start running, it will be fun for a long period of time. To gain maximum benefits from running, it is important to be regular at it. Like any other activity, listening to the same song, going to the office every morning or reading news, running may also become boring at some point of time. I won't blame you, if like many runners; you also start feeling this way after few weeks of running regularly. Running like any other form of exercise can get monotonous. Therefore, it is important to know how to spice it up so you don't lose the fire.

In this section, I have listed down a lot of ideas which will help you in making your runs entertaining and/or educational. The idea is to keep your runs as entertaining or educational as possible so that you can go out to run without fail and always look forward to your next run. Imagine, going out for a run and by the time you are back, you have learned something new.

I have tried many of the ideas listed below and even now use it as a tool to enhance my runs. Few ideas have been very helpful and I am glad I tried them. I would highly recommend you to try these and discover the one which suits you best. You may want to try all or few of the ideas before deciding.

Prerequisites (for first three): Smartphone/iPod/any portable audio device/etc.

Until and unless you are not running on a treadmill with a screen in front of it, audio is going to be your next best friend while running.

It is easy to setup and won't distract you from your surroundings. While your eyes are on the road, your mind is absorbing all the sound coming out of an earphone. I have a basic smartphone and have used it effectively to make all my runs as productive and enjoyable as possible.

1. Music: I had read somewhere that music increases running performance by up to 15%. That's an impressive figure. If listening to music while running can enhance your performance, then why not try some pumping music. I am a big fan of trance and have listened to many trance tracks during my runs. Send me a personal message and I will share the name of my favourite band. I even have a playlist which I use quite often whenever I feel like quitting a run. It helps me get back into the running groove!

2. Podcasts: This has been my favourite idea till date. I love it so much that I have promoted for free many of the episodes of the podcast to my friends and relatives. I have completed numerous series of podcasts while running and there was a time when I was obsessed with podcasts. Normally a podcast is 15-45 min long; therefore, I looked at every run as an opportunity to listen to a new episode. The motivation to listen to the next episode of a series is enough to push you to wear your running shoes and go out to run.

Podcasts not only make your run enjoyable but also productive and the best part is that almost all podcasts are free to download.

Check out the podcast sections on iTunes or Google music for a vast directory of podcasts and select your favorite genre. You can also explore podcast directories like Stitcher.

3. Audiobooks: I have completed an audiobook while running. This makes your runs hyper-productive and engaging. Imagine

finishing a book of your choice while running. If the book is engaging enough, then you will never want to stop running.

There are many resources from where you can download or stream audiobooks. Recommended websites are Audiobooks and Audible.

4. Run with someone: Human beings are social animals and if you are running with a companion, it makes running enjoyable. You will not just feel responsible to run regularly but you may also develop a good bond with your running companion. It could be the perfect date with your better half. It is definitely a good time to talk when both of you are feeling positive about yourself. If not your better half, go on and catch hold of any of your family members or a close friend who is interested in running with you. Initially, because of low stamina, you may struggle to mix talking and running at the same time. Within few days/weeks as you build your running stamina, talking at a normal pace will become easier.

Alternatively, if you have a dog at home, it can be a fun idea to run along with it. Both you and your dog will become fit.

5. Treat yourself: Another way to enjoy your runs is to treat yourself at regular intervals. Divide your big targets into smaller ones. Achieve these small targets and treat yourself - gift yourself something, eat something which you have been craving for a long time, take a short trip somewhere or spend quality time with your family or friends. The list is endless. This will help you stay motivated and you would want to earn more of the goodies.

Be creative when it comes to enjoying your runs. I have tried many tricks in the book and have come up with the above ideas which I found to be quite effective. Let me know if you have found some other way to enjoy your runs. I would be happy to try it and include it in any of the updated versions of this book for everyone's benefit.

BEST TIME TO RUN

"I don't find time to run, I make time to run."

Importance of no schedule

Assuming you have just started running (or thinking of starting), let me give you a very useful advice.

Run without a schedule!

Yes, you read it right.

You must have heard a lot about the importance of a schedule and why you should stick to it. The problem initially with sticking to a schedule is that it is <u>easy to miss</u>. Let's say, you have decided to run every morning at 6, maybe 4 days a week. Due to common reasons like you slept late at night or accidentally snoozed your alarm; you may wake up late on a couple of days. Let me tell you what would happen next. You will tell yourself that as you have missed your run, you will try to compensate it next day. Obviously, there are other priorities in life as well. From my experience, next day never materializes.

My advice - don't have a schedule, don't fix a time. Just fix a rough number of days (say 4-5) that you will go out to run per week. Focus on the current week. Forget future and past. Say, starting this Sunday you have decided to run 4 days per week. **Try to run 4 days as soon as possible in that week. Don't keep it pending until the end of the week.** At the end of the week, we always face situations when we have lots of commitments to fulfill. Likes of going on a date or taking your car to a garage would always seem to hold a higher priority than running. You have to decide what to do in such situations of course. A word of caution: what might seem like an emergency can be a genuine emergency. For general emergencies like the TV is not working or you forgot to throw away the garbage, my advice is that you should go for a quick run and then continue with your perceived emergencies (please use your own discretion).

Also, I would advise you to run in the morning and be done with it for the rest of the day. Nonetheless, if you miss your morning run, go for a run any other time of the day - afternoon, evening, late night – whenever possible! In my initial running days, I had run at 5 in the morning and at 11 in the night. **Just make sure to run any time of the day.** Don't let your mind play a game with you by saying that it is too late or too early. Just run!

If you are out of town for few days, remember to carry along a pair of running shoes and sportswear. In 2015, while I was on a vacation in India, in the evening, before hitting the pubs, I used to take out my running shoe and go out for a quick run. It is always a fulfilling feeling to run in a new city.

Try to run whenever and wherever possible, so that you keep on achieving your weekly targets.

Please, keep in mind your own safety. If it's dangerous to go out and run at 3 in the morning or in a particular locality, then simply don't do it. Use situational wisdom.

Importance of schedule

Once, you have got used to running say 4 days a week without any proper time schedule, you will start noticing something very interesting. Your body and mind will automatically align to a time of the day when you can run most effectively. You will sense it yourself. It happens quite often. I understood after a few weeks of running regularly that my runs are most effective in the evenings. I have often run in the evenings after sunset as I understood my natural body clock and when I can perform best. I know many fitness trainers would recommend running in the morning as your body would continue to burn calories throughout the day and you get a good night's sleep. Honestly, your body will tell you what to do. Listen to it; it is way smarter than you think. Happy discovering!

USEFUL TOOLS

"The tools which would teach men their own use would be beyond price."
- Plato (Classical Greek philosopher)

Shoes

Probably, the most important tool for running is an investment in a good pair of shoes. A proper shoe will not only reduce the chances of injuries but will also provide proper grip and support. A good pair of shoes will reduce the impact on the knee joints. I have listed below a rough guideline in order to help you identify a proper pair of shoes for yourself:

1. Determine the kind of surface you intend to run on most of the days: This will help you decide the extent of traction needed in your shoes along with the level of cushioning required. In general, people run on surfaces like road, track or treadmill. Harder the surface, more cushioning is required.

2. Types of foot: There are 3 main categories of foot-types - Neutral footed, over-pronation and under-pronation. In layman's language, it is your footprint. When you walk or run, as per your foot's bone structure, your strides leave an unseen mark on the floor.

3. Wet-test: To know your foot type, take a piece of paper and die your foot with water/ink/colour. Place your foot on the paper like a normal step. Now google over-pronation or under-pronation and match the mark. This way you can identify your foot type.

4. The Final Step - Buying the footwear: I know, from my own experience, that online shopping has its own perks in terms of discounts and the comfort of ordering from home or office. Having said that, I would still advise you to visit a nearby shoe store to buy your running shoe. It is important to understand the feel of the shoe before using it. Also, the staff at the store will be able to help you select the perfect shoe. Tell the salesperson the surface you want to run on and your type of foot. You will get better options to choose from and will save time. My personal favorites are Nike and Adidas running shoes.

Remember, you need your pair of shoes for the next 400-500 miles, so, invest wisely!

If you still wish to purchase your pair of running shoes online, then please feel free to explore them. You can find few affiliate links on my website, MadOverRunning (www.madoverrunning.com).

Mobile Apps

Today, there are multiple mobile apps available to tracks all your runs. I have listed below few of my personal favorites:

1. Nike running app: I have been using this app since the beginning of my running journey and love it.
Download links: Android/iOS.

I love this app mainly because of its two major features. First, it has inbuilt training plans for all formats of long runs like 5k, 10k, half-marathon, etc. This means that once you download this app, you need not look any further for training plans. Second, it's free.

The disadvantage is that it is a pure running app and just in case you want to cycle or dance on a particular day, you won't be able to switch to cycle/dance mode and track it.

2. Runtastic: Another app which I have tried in my initial running days. This app was recommended to me by a friend back in college. The benefit of this app over the Nike app is that you will be able to switch easily between running/cycling/walking/other forms. It tracks all your activities no matter what it is.
There are many more features in this app which are quite useful. The only catch is that to avail most of the useful features you have to pay. You can also join a training program but for that again, you have to pay a one-time fee of approximately $20. It's still worth it.
Download links: Android/iOS.

3. Adidas train & run: I have never used it but the features look pretty cool. I would love to hear your feedback in case you happen to use it.
Download links: Android/iOS.

All of the above apps are nice and work effectively. I will leave the options for your discretion. If you want to explore more apps in addition to the ones that I have mentioned then please feel free to do so.

Gears

Quick disclaimer: Not all suggestions mentioned below are necessary for running. Remember, the lesser you carry, the better your runs will be. This applies to your body as well. I am talking about that extra flab if you didn't get it at the first instance.

The items listed below are unique in their own way of usage. Whether you think that it is important for you while running is absolutely your choice and I do not want to influence it in any way. I am merely sharing my experience with different products which have I tried during the course of last few years. As we go through the list, I will share the merits and demerits so that it's easy for you to decide. You may find a lot of people using few/all of the gears in their runs. Please refrain from mindlessly copying anyone or following just for the heck of it. The only time you will look cool is when you are able to run effortlessly. If you feel that you need a particular product, then do not be shy and go ahead to try it.

1. Clothing: This is important. It is not about looking good. Proper clothing is often neglected by many first time runners. I am guilty as well and later on realised that I should have taken care of it long time back. The clothes you wear at the time of running should be very comfortable. In a run, you sweat, you get warm, you constantly try to maintain correct posture and try to keep yourself focused. The last thing which you want is distracting from your run is improper clothing. It is directly linked to your running performance.

Wear clothes made of good materials. I am not an expert on various fabrics used in the manufacturing processes but a well-branded sportswear is generally a safe bet. Avoid bulky clothes made of thick materials. My personal favorites are Nike/Adidas t-shirts and shorts. A comfortable pair of sports socks is important. You need the kind of socks which will be able to absorb sweat and create a good grip on the inside surface of your shoe. Additionally, a padded pair of socks helps absorb the impact of running every time your foot hits the surface.
You have to buy only once and you will be able to focus on your runs quite comfortably for a long period of time. I have been using a pair of blue coloured Adidas running shorts for past 3 years and it still feels new. The best shorts that I have ever bought.

Take special care of your undergarments. For women, it is advisable to use a sports bra. Loose undergarments will hurt private body parts while running.

Visit a sports shop nearby to explore all the options. Remember that it has to be light and should be able to wick sweat.
Invest in your clothes.

You can purchase online from the following affiliate link: MadOverRunning (https://www.madoverrunning.com/resource)

1. Fitness bands: Nowadays, a lot of high tech fitness bands are available in the market. If you wish, you can buy a fitness band according to your budget. My personal experience says that a simple smartphone is also good enough. Buying a fitness band is a personal choice, the decision of which I will again leave up to you. It is surely more convenient as compared to carrying a smartphone. Please just don't buy a heavy fitness band as it will bother you

while running. Fitbit, Garmin have established names in the industry. My mother uses Xiaomi Mi band to track her evening walks and it works just fine. It is also one of the cheapest options and I guess at the end of the day, what's most important is how much money are you are willing to spend and the features which you are looking for.

You can purchase it from the following affiliate link: MadOverRunning (https://www.madoverrunning.com/resource)

2. Armband: If you are going to use a smartphone to track your runs or listen to some audio, then an armband is pretty useful. In the beginning, it is a bit uncomfortable and you may take some time to adjust. You can simply wrap it around your arm and then your hands are free. It is a low-cost product that won't burn a hole in your pocket so don't overthink if you want to try it out. I prefer holding my phone in the hands, switching from left to right.

You can purchase it from the following affiliate link: MadOverRunning (https://www.madoverrunning.com/resource)

3. Earphones: If you are running outside or prefer listening to the audio of your choice inside a gym then, it is best to use a sports earphone as opposed to a regular earphone for clear sound. Sports earphones are ideally sweat proof. There are many products on the market which cater to this need.

You can purchase it from the following affiliate link: MadOverRunning (https://www.madoverrunning.com/resource)

4. Water container: I don't think you need to worry much about dehydration until and unless you are running more than 5 km at a stretch. Nonetheless, it's always good to carry a small bottle in case you feel thirsty. Don't gulp lots of water during your runs, few sips every 15-20 min should be enough.

You can purchase it from the following affiliate link:
MadOverRunning (https://www.madoverrunning.com/resource)

5. YouTube: Continued learning opens up the mind. There are many instructional videos by experts and enthusiasts to help you with getting in-depth knowledge and useful tips regarding running. I have watched numerous YouTube videos to understand proper running postures, diet, tips, and tricks.
You can view my favourite YouTube videos at the following link:
MadOverRunning (https://www.madoverrunning.com/resource)

6. Marathon Websites: There are tons of websites that come out with blog posts and articles to help you with running. You may want to subscribe to few in order to get regular updates. I regularly publish blogs as well and would welcome you to join the community.
Few of my favorite websites can be found in the following link:
MadOverRunning (https://www.madoverrunning.com/resource)

7. Podcasts: As mentioned earlier in the 'How to enjoy Running' section, you can use podcasts to educate yourself. Subscribe to podcast channels from the running genre and gain knowledge on the go. You will get to listen to interviews of people who have already done it, discussions on useful topics and updates on global running events.
Few of my favorites are mentioned in the following link:
MadOverRunning (https://www.madoverrunning.com/resource)

8. Books: The current book which you are reading is perfect for beginners. Additionally, it will also help those who are a bit experienced. If even after reading this book you desire to gain more knowledge, then be assured that there are hundreds of books available in every marketplace.

You can purchase one from the following affiliate link: [MadOverRunning](https://www.madoverrunning.com/resource)

Feel free to order any of the books mentioned above and get more insight about the topic.

While you are thinking of trying the above tools, let me remind you once again that these are just tools. What's more important is execution. Running is a low demanding exercise. You need not buy fancy stuff to go out and run. It is one of the simplest forms of exercise. Few people like to shop. I have often noticed that new runners start buying/trying new things which are available in the market and end up either never or seldom using them. The reason is that they quit running. When you are not running regularly, then these tools just sit idle in the closet or on your desk. The one thing which you need to remind yourself time and again is that running regularly is most important of all. Some of the tools mentioned above may make sense to you. Choose wisely.

CORRECT RUNNING POSTURE

"A good stance and posture reflect a proper state of mind."
- Morihei Ueshiba (Founder of Aikido)

Importance of breathing properly

Breathing properly is one of the most important aspects of efficient running. Long-time back, a trainer taught me that if we can learn and take control of our breathing pattern then excelling in any form of sports is not difficult. Obviously, you need to learn the skills as well but breathing can help you become a top performer. A regular supply of oxygen-rich air is essential for sustained performance. Try to understand your breathing pattern and learn to control it in order to become a better athlete.

There has always been an argument between breathing through the nose versus breathing through the mouth. So, which one is better? I guess the best answer lies with you. Your body constantly tells you what needs to be done. When I started running a few years ago, I was mostly inhaling air through my mouth. With time, as my stamina increased, I started breathing through the nose as well. It was an automatic transition from mouth breathing to nose breathing. As your running stamina increases, your body starts using less amount of oxygen for the same intensity of the workout. You won't totally stop mouth breathing. Even now, I switch to mouth breathing when I am running hard or have covered a lot of distance. Your body will tell you how much oxygen it needs. I just follow what my body tells me to do. Trust me, it is the best judge. I don't even have to think about it. It is so spontaneous and natural.

My advice for you is to allow your body to decide and not to force anything. Hey! You are just starting out. All you need to focus on is going out regularly and run. Don't split your brain thinking about the breathing techniques at this stage. If you start panting while running and it gets uncomfortable, try to walk a bit or simply stop. Take it easy my friends, take it easy. With time, as you run more often, you will gain control over your breathing.

The key thing to remember is to "**listen to your body**".

Posture

Maintaining a proper posture while running will not only help you become a better runner but also avoid injuries. As kids, all of us had learned the correct postures of standing, sitting, walking and 'running'. Now is the time to implement those good habits. Straight back, relaxed shoulders, arms to your side (don't swing too much), chest out and head pointing straight ahead (don't look down). Try to maintain this correct posture throughout your run and you will be able to run effectively.

I have seen that many individuals have a tendency to look down while running. This may partially block your windpipe which results in improper breathing.

Another observation is that after running a substantial distance, my back tends to slouch due to tiredness. This is a bad posture for running and you should keep an eye on it. Consciously straighten your back when this happens. In a later chapter, I will tell you how to make your back (core) strong. Strengthening your core will help maintain correct posture for a longer period of time while running.

What you should not do

Here is a list of things that you should not do before, during or after running:

Before a run:

1. Do not overstretch. A little bit of stretching is fine, though.

2. Do not eat or drink much. I would advise eating at least 2 hours before running. Do not drink lots of water before running. It's difficult to run with a partially full stomach.

3. Don't go for a run if you are feeling dehydrated. It is better to have a glass of water and wait for half an hour before going out for a run. Running is a sweaty affair. A dehydrated body will make things worse and can also prove to be detrimental to your health.

4. This one is huge. I learned it by committing a mistake. DO NOT buy a new pair of shoes few days before the marathon. Our feet take some time to get used to the new pair of shoes. This 'getting-used-to a new shoe' duration hampers your performance right before the marathon. I bought a new pair of shoes a couple of days before a half-marathon. For a week, my running performance had decreased. My feet would start aching after 1-2 km. Eventually, I had to switch back to my old pair of shoes and interestingly, everything was back to normal and I could run comfortably again. If you urgently need a new pair of shoes, I would strongly advise changing it after the marathon day. For running a race use the same pair of shoes which you used during your training. It is wise to start with a new pair of shoes at the beginning of the training or after the marathon.

During a run:

1. Do not look down while running. As explained earlier, this will cause partial windpipe blockage and you won't be able to inhale and exhale efficiently.

2. Do not sip in lots of water while running. Your stomach will get full and it will be difficult to continue running. Few sips here and there are fine.

3. Do not swing your arms a lot while running, you will only waste your energy. The idea is to conserve as much energy as possible while running. However, it is also imperative to keep it natural and not to self-impose stiff arms.

4. Do not slouch while running. It is common to return to our regular lazy slouch position after you have run few miles. Keep an eye on your posture and correct it whenever possible.

5. It is quite normal to feel a bit of pain in your calf muscles, thigh muscles or abdomen at the time of running. Discontinue running and walk or stop altogether. The pain will most probably be gone in a few minutes. If not, then, you should head back home and rest. Seek medical attention if the pain persists.

6. Listen to your body. It keeps sending small signals which, with time, you will be able to understand - tiredness, thirst, pain, adrenaline rush, anything and everything. Initially, don't push much and keep your runs as natural as possible - just listen to your body.

After a run:

1. Do not gulp in lots of water immediately. Slowly and steadily sip it all.

2. Do not eat as soon as you are done with running. Your body is heated up after a run. Let it cool down a bit. Let it relax. At the same time, if you are very hungry, use situational wisdom by eating a little bit.

3. Do not take a shower as soon as your run is over. As mentioned earlier, your body is warm and it's best if you allow it to cool down a bit. Take shower to clean yourself, not to bring down your body temperature. Pour some water on your head to feel refreshed.

4. Do not immediately drink alcohol. Alcohol can dehydrate your body. At the same time if you are in a situation where you can't say no then at least give yourself enough time to recover the lost water.

MOTIVATION

"Only I can change my life. No one can do it for me."
- Carol Burnett (American actress, comedian, singer and writer)

How much do you need?

Human beings are moody. At times we may feel so motivated that we would not even think twice before attempting to run 10 km and on the other hand, there may be times when getting out of the bed in the morning may seem a humongous task. There are two types of motivation, namely internal and external.

Internal motivation arises from a strong 'Why', which we have already covered at the beginning of the book. External motivation has the power to ignite your internal motivation. Be careful here, if you are depending a lot on external motivation triggers then probably your internal motivation is not so strong enough. It is only human to be in the midst of a cloudy mind every now and then. Many external circumstances and triggers like office stress, a family vacation, disturbed personal life and the likes can distract us and we tend to lose our internal motivation. At such times we need some sort of external motivation. I have used various methods to keep myself motivated few of which I will share with you in this section.

Only you can decide how much motivation is needed by you. Few people may have a very strong 'Why' and staying motivated may not be an issue for them. For others, constant external motivation may be an essential requirement. It doesn't matter what the ratio of internal to external motivation is, what matters most is the end result. Are you running regularly and achieving your goals? In my initial running days, I had watched many motivational YouTube videos mostly because I was too lazy to go out and run. Right before a run, I used to watch a small motivational video. Even today, sometimes I listen to adrenaline-pumping music to boost my runs. Sometimes, I remind myself why I love running.

Today, running has become a habit and I do not need much of the external motivation. My days feel incomplete if I miss my runs.

Below, I have listed a few resources to keep you motivated.

1. YouTube: As mentioned earlier in this section, YouTube is a great resource for motivational videos. Being the second largest search engine after Google, this platform has a plethora of motivational videos to keep your spirits high.

2. Music: Music has the power to enhance your running performance by up to 15%. You may remember this statistic from a previous section. If you have ever been to a gym, you must have heard some groovy beats. They understand the power of good music. Search for some good music and use it in your runs.

3. Before-after success stories: It is always motivating to know some inspirational before-after success stories. If you catch hold of such stories then dig deep and try to figure out the core motivation behind these mind-boggling transformations. You will also observe that in most of the cases the desire to succeed was very strong. Not all of the advice which you will read or hear maybe suitable for you. Try to customize the lessons as per your running regime and fitness goals.

4. Talk to someone who has already run a marathon: If you know someone who has already run a half-marathon/marathon, then probably they have faced similar challenges. Talk to them and learn from their mistakes. Today, I can confidently talk about running because I have overcome all the struggles and have finally succeeded in it. Running events and social media platforms are great connecting points. You can follow me on [Quora](https://www.quora.com/profile/Kanisk-Nayan) where I regularly answer queries related to running and training.

DIET

"Abs are made in the kitchen."

What to eat and what not to eat?

A good diet plays a significant role in overall fitness. Eat right and you will see good results in a very short span of time. You will feel more energetic and will be at your fittest possible avatar. Eat wrong and you will always be low on energy and the desired results will be achieved in a comparatively long period of time.

As a beginner, drastically changing your diet is not at all advisable but there are certainly few tips that you can be mindful of:

1. Processed food is not healthy, no matter what the advertisements tell you and the number of nutrients the package mentions.

2. Eat fresh vegetables and fruits as much as possible.

Few worthy mentions for runners: Below mentioned are not essential but are better than other options because of their nutritional value content. Ideally, you should mix all types of vegetables and fruits in your diet.

Vegetables	Fruits
Kale, Cucumber, Tomato, Carrot, Spinach, Radish	Banana, Orange, Avocado, Pomegranate

1. Create a diet consisting of different food groups - Fruits, vegetables, grains, cereals, meat, milk products, etc. If your food is COLORFUL (not artificial colors), most certainly it is healthy. Vegetables and fruits get their colour from plant pigments. These pigments have antioxidant. Antioxidants are good for your body as they provide free electrons which in turn neutralize free radicals in your body i.e. antioxidants prevent oxidation of molecules and any potential harm to cellular structures. Don't worry if you didn't get it. Just know that it's good and by eating a variety of fruits and vegetables you will remain healthy.

2. Avoid fast (read junk) foods - Yes, I know that you already are already aware of the fact that fast foods were never good for your health. I am not recommending you to completely refrain from eating fast foods. Once in a while should be fine as long as you are running regularly. After all, our taste buds need cheat days as well. I love Indian fast foods but at the same time, I keep a tab on the frequency and quantity. Most of the times I do a subconscious evaluation of the fast food before having it. Most of the fast foods are rich in trans-fat and low on nutrition. Regular intakes of fast foods lead to obesity, diabetes and other lifestyle diseases. Next time if there is an urge to eat fast food, try to say no and remind yourself of all the hard work you are putting in to get fit.

3. Protein - As we run, our muscles regularly wear and tear. To build them back, our bodies need proteins which help in the recovery of muscles. Few examples of protein-rich foods are listed below. These are natural food items and can be easily found in your local market.

Vegetarian sources	Non-vegetarian sources
Milk, yogurt, pulses, soy, almonds, oats, cottage cheese, broccoli, peanuts.	Meat, eggs, seafood, lean beef, tuna

If you are short of time, you can also try Whey protein. You may purchase it from the following affiliate link: MadOverRunning (https://www.madoverrunning.com/resource). For your kind information, whey is a type of protein details of which is out of the scope of this book. For your reference, you may like to read more about it here (https://en.wikipedia.org/wiki/Whey).

Based on your cultural food habit, you can easily judge what healthy and unhealthy foods are. *Tasty food is not always healthy but you can always make healthy food tasty.* For example, I am an Indian and belong to Eastern part of the country. Rice is a staple food for my family. I love eating rice but for the sake of staying fit, I try to control the amount of rice intake. Also, spicy and oily food is a routine in my family. I make sure that I stay in control of what I eat. You are the best auditor of your eating habit.

When you start running regularly, something amazing happens. As mentioned earlier, you will subconsciously start keeping a check on your eating habit. A normal conversation which runs in my mind is - "Kanisk, you are training so hard. Please don't ruin it by eating rubbish. Eat healthy food! Eat healthy food!"

What to eat after a run?

After a long run, your body has lost water and essential nutrients. It is important to refuel it as soon as possible. Ideally, you should eat something within 30 minutes post workout.

Additionally, eating within 30 minutes can reduce the chances of muscle stiffness and soreness.

So, the important question one should ask is - What should be eaten after a run?

Rule of thumb: 1 portion of protein to 3 portions of carbohydrates (1:3). Ideal numbers are close to 20 g of protein to 60 g of carbohydrates.

You need not eat a full meal right after your run but essential proteins and carbohydrates can be taken in the suggested ratio. If you don't feel like eating right after your run, then drinking something can be a good alternative.

Few worthy mentions:

Vegetarian	Drink
Nutrition bars work just fine. Clif bars or Power bars are few healthy options. Look for bars with protein to carbohydrates ratio as 1:3. Bagel with peanut butter. Sandwich with lean meat, eggs, or low-fat cheese. Greek yogurt, granola, and mixed berries. Fruit and yogurt smoothie. E.g. Banana and yogurt smoothie.	500 ml of chocolate milk. Chocolate milk provides plenty of protein, carbohydrates and Vitamin B. Whey protein shake.

After a rigorous workout (be it of any form), small amounts of high-GI carbohydrates like potatoes, pasta, bread, and rice are good choices for refueling muscles.

Quick fact: GI stands for the glycaemic index (GI). It is the food's effect on a person's blood glucose level. It is commonly referred to as blood sugar level. Pure glucose is indicated by 100 which represents pure glucose (reference source, https://en.wikipedia.org/wiki/Glycemic_index).

Therefore, if you are taking high GI carbohydrates then it means that blood glucose can be easily refueled in the body.

A bigger meal can be taken about 1-2 hours post workout and you can continue to eat something every 2-3 hours for the rest of the day.

Recovery basics - '**The Four R's**'.

Rest - Get a good night's sleep. This is when most of your muscles will be repaired.

Rehydrate - Replace fluid losses by drinking water and healthy beverages at regular intervals throughout the day.

Repair - Have protein and carbohydrates in the ratio of 20g:60g within 30 minutes post workout to kick-start muscle repair.

Refuel - Eat carbohydrates to help restore energy.

A good practice is to weigh yourself before and after a workout. For every pound (453.6 g) lost, you should consume an equivalent amount of water or sports drink.

Hydration

When running we lose water in the form of sweat. It is important that we stay hydrated throughout the day. I have listed down some points to be kept in mind:

General day-to-day hydration tips:

1. Drink a glass of water right after you wake up in the morning. We dehydrate in our sleep and it is always good to have a glass of

water early morning before taking in your regular cup of coffee/tea.

2. Drink water at regular intervals throughout the day. You can aim to intake approximately 2 liters of water a day.

Hydration tips while running:

1. Short runs (<5K): Soon after your run, slowly sip in a glass of water. This helps in re-hydrating your body at the earliest.

2. Long runs (>5K): Chocolate milk, salty lemon water would be apt for recovery.

3. Packed fruit juices available at your local market are not just processed but also contain sugar. If you still want to buy one for yourself then look for labels saying '100% fruit juice'. Everything else contains artificial sugar. As much as possible, drink freshly squeezed fruit juices.

4. When it comes to alcohol, it's a personal choice. At the same time, it's good to remember that alcohol can be dehydrating if taken in excess. To compensate this, it is advisable to drink enough water in between your drinks – even then, drinking more water won't be able to compensate for the dehydration. The problem with alcohols is that it affects *antidiuretic hormones* (ADH) production in the body, something that helps in regulating urine frequency. In layman's words, alcohol messes with its production and therefore we tend to pee more during and after drinking.

Also, frequent drinking can lead to accumulation of fat in the body. I have learned over the years of social drinking that Vodka Soda, both Red & White Wine, Bloody Mary, Whisky, Scotch, Bourbon (on the rocks or with water) are fairly healthier options. WHO recommends no more than 1 drink a day for women and 2 drinks per day for men. While I am not advocating daily drinking, I want you to understand is that you can control the calorie intake when it comes to alcohol as well. Go on and explore the internet, I am sure you will find a low-calorie drink as per your liking.

CROSS-TRAINING

"Life begins at the end of your comfort zone."

As mentioned earlier, no exercise is complete in itself. The same principle applies to running as well. It is important to include some cross training exercises in your regime. You may frown and ask, "More exercise in addition to running?"

For your benefit, the answer is YES!

I would suggest you focus more on strengthening the core. The core is the midsection of your body which includes front, back and side muscles. These work as 'Stabilizing Muscles' for the whole body and play an important role in the daily routine. A strong core can help you with correct posture and provide extra strength while running. With a rise of a sedentary lifestyle, we are rather compelled to sit for long hours at work or school. This lifestyle has forced on us an average of 8-10 hours daily sitting sessions with very limited time for physical activity. The human body is not designed to be seated for long durations. It is built for activity. Strengthening the core has become more of a necessity than choice today's age of inactivity.

A major benefit of 'cross-training' or strengthening the core is that it helps in avoiding injuries. Over a period of time, your whole body benefits from a strong core. There are close to 650-850 muscles in our body and running alone can't get all those muscles strong. When you cross train, a lot more muscles are used and over a period of time, your running performance gets better. Like other forms of exercises even running is not complete.

Some recommended cross-training exercises: Yoga, Swimming, Walking, Hiking, Cycling, Zumba, Sports, etc.

Few recommended core exercises: Planks, Side planks, Russian twists, Lunges, Superman, Push-ups, Leg raises, etc.

For starters, include cross-training exercise at least once a week. It's definitely fun to mix up your running regime with cross training as it breaks the monotonous running routine.

INJURIES

"Injuries, burns, and bruises will heal but victory lasts forever."
- Phillipe Nover (Retired American Mixed martial artist)

Different types of injuries you should know about

Disclaimer: *I am not a medical practitioner nor do I claim to be a sports injury expert. Below mentioned information related to injuries is only a general guideline and I would advise you to consult a doctor for accurate information.*

Awareness of the types of injuries is as crucial as treatment.

1. **Runner's knee** - Running is a high impact sport and can hurt your knees if proper attention and care are not taken. After running my first half-marathon, my knees were mildly hurting for next few hours. Prior to that, I had never felt any sort of pain in my knees.

How to avoid it: Wear a well-cushioned pair of shoes. Also, if possible run on soft surfaces like, grass, rubber tracks, loose soil, beach, etc. There is something known as GRF (ground reaction force). It is the equal and opposite force which we feel as a result of foot strike. I hope it is obvious now that a softer surface means lower GRF. Also, a cushioned pair of shoes helps in absorbing the impact. Therefore, a soft surface combined with a pair of cushioned shoes is the best thing you can do for your knees.

2. **Shin splint**: Shin bone is the front facing bone that connects the knee to the sole. If you run regularly and a good distance every week, then at times you may feel pain in this part of the leg. It can be a temporary harmless pain or a shin splint. When you feel any pain then ideally you should stop and take few moments of rest.

Alternatively, you could switch to walking for some time. If it subsides then its normal pain otherwise it could be a shin splint.

How to avoid it: Do not jump into extensive running too soon. Gradually increase your endurance so that your body adjusts at its own natural pace.

3. **Bloody nipples**: Ouch! Yes, it hurts. While running, our nipples rub against the t-shirt and because of friction, it may start bleeding. I was so afraid of this phenomenon in the first half-marathon that I wore two layers of t-shirts. Just in case it happened, hopefully, no one would have been able to see it. Women are fortunate in this case as they can have a layer of padded sports bra between their nipples and the t-shirt. Men are not so lucky. If you are a guy then you may want to try cotton vests. Having said that I am not too sure if it works. Let me know if you feel any difference after using it.

How to avoid it: Before going out for a run you can paste a Band-Aid over your nipples. Also, I would advise you to wear high-quality t-shirts which are designed to wick sweat. Other popular ideas are 'nip guards' and 'bodyglide' (a deodorant stick like product which after application to any particular body part would keep it smooth for a certain time period).

You can purchase it one from the following link: MadOverRunning (https://www.madoverrunning.com/resource)

4. **Chafing/blisters**: This type of skin irritation is the result of friction between the skin and any clothing.

How to avoid it: If your current t-shirt and pair of shorts are not suitable for running, then you may try a different fabric. Probably, you are wearing the wrong fabric. Another tip is that before going out for a run you can apply petroleum jelly or talcum powder to the most prone area.

At any point of running if you feel extreme pain or discomfort, please visit your doctor immediately.

At the early stages of running, above-mentioned injuries are rare. You may feel a bit of a pain in either of the legs initially but that is most probably temporary and should be gone soon. As you get regular with running, your muscles will get stronger and pain will become less frequent.

No pain no gain

A bit of shift in the mindset will help bear initial pain related to running with a smile. Running is a high impact exercise and may cause some kind of pain. Know that little bit of pain in the initial running days is indicating that your muscles are working out. They wear and tear and recover every day. During the process of muscle recovery, you become stronger and fitter. A quick note on being mindful of the pain and if you feel uncomfortable then seek medical attention.

REGISTERING FOR HALF-MARATHON

"Every accomplishment starts with the decision to try."
-Gail Devers (American retired track and field athlete)

Declaration to the world

Let me give you a quick tip to run your first half-marathon. Declare it to the world! Tell your family members and close friends. Psychologically, when you share a decision with someone a sense of responsibility seeps in. At the back of your mind, a general self-conversation is - "I have declared it to so many people and they will surely ask me about it in future. I have to do it". At the same time, I would also recommend you do not feel any undue pressure because of this. It's ok if due to some reason or the other you are unable to run a half-marathon. Be proud of yourself if at least you tried. The majority of the population doesn't even think about it.

Take help from support groups

I cannot forget this part of my training. A very close friend of mine was responsible for keeping me on track. I stay in India whereas she resides in the US. One day, I called her and asked her to become my unofficial mentor. She happily agreed and thereafter, every day, I used to report the number of miles that I had run. We used to talk on how to train, what to eat, various strategies, etc. She used to motivate me a lot and told me about people she knew who were in their forties and ran 8-10 miles at a stretch. I can never thank her enough.

It's always a good idea to get similar support from a family member, friend or any support group. Remember, we are social animals.

Training for half-marathon

There are many resources on how to train for half-marathon. This book should be enough for you to start your running journey. As mentioned earlier, the Nike app has a free half-marathon schedule. There are many free resources if you just Google.

If you are ready to shell out few bucks from your pocket, then there are many websites and mobile apps which are able to create a customized training schedule for you.

Few useful resources could be found in the following link: MadOverRunning (https://www.madoverrunning.com/resource)

Taking the first step (schedule)

Probably the section you have been waiting for. I have created a simple schedule for you to kick-start running. It is both simple and easy to follow.

Schedule for the first 1-2 months of training:

Step 1: Month 1

Target Distance: 1 mile (approx. 1.6 km)

Frequency: 4 days/week of running + 1 day for cross-training

Week 1: You need not run all the way. Mix your runs with a little bit of walk as well.

Week 2: Same distance and frequency as the first week but try to cover more distance now by running.

Week 3: Cover more distance by running rather than walking.

Week 4: Hopefully by the beginning of the 4th week, you are able to run one mile completely.

Your body should have got accustomed to running by now.

Step 2: Month 2

Distance: Gradually, start increasing distance every week. As a thumb rule, do not increase more than 10% from your last week's average distance. E.g. If last week, your average distance per run was 1 mile, then aim to run an increased average of 1.1 miles (=1 mile*1.1) this week. A week after that, the average distance should be 1.21 miles (=1.1 miles*1.1). So on and so forth. I hope you get the idea. Use the below formula to calculate your target distance every week:

*This week's distance = Last week's distance * 1.1*

Frequency: 4 days/week of running + 1 day for cross-training

Remember, slow and steady wins the race. Don't rush. Do not drastically increase the distance. Let your body settle into the new regime. It's perfectly alright if you are even able to run 1.5 miles (approx. 2.4 km) by the end of the second month. Just ensure that you are running at least 4 days a week.

The idea is to allow your body to get used to running regularly.

Step 3: Start half-marathon training

Register for a half-marathon and begin its training as advised by the mobile app or website of your choice. Stick to the schedule as recommended in the training plan and hit a home run on your first attempt. I am a satisfied customer of Nike mobile app for half-marathon training and would highly recommend it. Big fan!

Many running events have a deadline for finishing half-marathon mainly because the roads are blocked for the event and the permission is only for few hours. You are free to finish your run within the pre-decided target time. As a bonus, if you finish your run within a pre-decided target time, then you will get a timing certificate. For half-marathon, the time limit is generally three hours. Check the time limit in the terms and conditions section. There are many popular half-marathon events in the world which sell out very fast. If you don't register on time you may miss out on the slot and will have to try next year. Timing certificates are important in such situations since it acts as a qualifying certificate. Event organizers prefer to approve candidates who have some prior half-marathon experience.

At the end remember that if you train properly, eat well, rest well and believe in yourself, then you will be able to run and complete your first half-marathon.

"AT THE FINISH LINE, THERE IS LIFETIME GLORY!"

FINAL WORDS FROM THE AUTHOR

"If you align your expectations with reality, you will never be disappointed."
- Terrell Owens (former American footballer)

I love running and even after publicly displaying my love for it, I have to include this section. As mentioned a few times earlier, running in itself is not a complete exercise and it has its own limitations. Few of the points may be repeated as a gentle reminder.

Realistic expectations from running:

1. Let me be honest with you, running alone won't transform your body into a well-carved physique like that of Sylvester Stallone from the movie Rocky. For that to happen you need to hit the gym. All forms of exercises/sports have their own benefits and limitations. It is always best to mix exercises for maximum results.

2. Running is a high impact exercise. Like any other type of sports, there are chances of injury. As mentioned in an earlier section, after running my first half-marathon I experienced for the first time in my running journey knee pain. I was terrified. It is said that after running a full marathon, we lose few centimeters of height because of the high impact. The good news is that we get back to our original height in few hours. Don't be scared. Even though running is a great exercise, I recommend you to mix various forms of exercises. This way extensive running won't damage your body. Also, it's good to remember that it takes years of incorrect running form to hurt your knees permanently. Follow a good running

posture and take proper diet to heal yourself at the earliest. Proper rest is an important aspect of running which many people ignore. To reduce knee impact, run on soft surfaces like grass, rubber track and use a well-cushioned pair of shoes.

3. Running can get boring after a certain point in time. Imagine you are running continuously for 30-45 min. It gets even more boring if you are running on a treadmill or in circles of a track. You can try audio entertainment as mentioned in a previous section to tackle this problem.

4. Many times you are running all alone. Honestly, I love it. In this busy world, we hardly get time for ourselves. I see running as an opportunity to do some self-talk and plan things. I have reflected a lot of my life while running. I have thought of how things are, how things should be and how to work on it. Running is the perfect brainstorming session. Our greatest ideas come to us when the mind is free and that certainly happens with me while running.

THANK YOU

Congratulations! You have made it so far. If you read the book completely, your head must be filled with a to-do-list. It is now time to take action. If you already feel an adrenaline rush with the idea of running, don't stop yourself and go out for a run! If at the moment you can't go out to run, then do 20 push-ups. Do something to calm you down. Get into the 'action' mode. Don't think, act. Don't be, do.

I hope that you have enjoyed reading this book as much I have enjoyed writing it. I have put in a lot of time and effort to create it and would appreciate if you would not share your copy with your friends/relatives without my consent. Although I would encourage you to share the following link with someone who you feel can benefit from this book. They can buy it from various marketplaces, the links of which could be found on the dedicated website - https://www.madoverrunning.com.

I hope you would agree with me that word of mouth is still the best form of advertisement. I would kindly request you to leave an honest review at the marketplace from where you bought this book.

Feel free to follow me on various social media platforms - Facebook, Twitter, Google Plus and Goodreads.

I wish you all the best for your first 5K/10K/half-marathon. Share your progress with me. In case of any queries, please feel free to reach out to me on Twitter (@kanisknayan) and I will be happy to answer.

Stay fit, stay blessed!

THE END

Printed in Great Britain
by Amazon